FINISHING LINE PRESS

www.finishinglinepress.com

Yesterday Echoes

poems by

Chris Wood

Finishing Line Press
Georgetown, Kentucky

Yesterday Echoes

*This book is dedicated to all those who came before me
and shaped who I am today.*

ACKNOWLEDGMENTS

With gratitude, I am pleased to acknowledge the following publications where my work originally appeared, sometimes in slightly different forms:

American Diversity Report: "Sweet Harvest"
An Introverts Tour: An Anthology by Poetry World: "Buried Driveway"
Chattanooga Writers' Guild: "Abandoned to the Interstate"
Dragonfly Arts Magazine: "Home Remedy"
Heart of Flesh Literary Journal: "The Long Remembering"
Imspired: "Scent of Smoke"
In Parentheses: "Betrayal"
Lit Shark Magazine: "When Daffodils Sing" and "Camping at Dale Hollow Lake"
Lucky Jefferson: "Planted for Me"
Mildren Haun Review: "She Does Everything, Says Nothing," "Under the Swing Set," and "When I Was Eight"
Monterey Poetry Review: "Spring Libations"
Poetry As Promised Magazine: "Dad's Pipe" and "Suppertime"
Poetry Quarterly: "Every Visit to the Dry Cleaners" and "Yesterday Echoes"
Quill and Parchment: "He Says Nothing, Does Everything"
Rainbow Poems: "In the Middle of Things"
Salvation South: "Basic Recipe for Squash," "Birthplace," "Canning," "Heritage," and "Remembering the Farm Girl"

Publisher: Leah Huete de Maines
Editor: Christen Kincaid
Cover Art: Chris Wood
Author Photo: Chris Wood
Cover Design: Elizabeth Maines McCleavy

Order online: www.finishinglinepress.com
also available on amazon.com

Author inquiries and mail orders:
Finishing Line Press
PO Box 1626
Georgetown, Kentucky 40324
USA

Contents

Introduction

Yesterday echoes in each of us. Cherished memories hidden beneath the surface only to be revealed through the power of sensory details that keeps the past alive even as time moves forward. A simple trip to the dry cleaners, a scar, or celebrating the beauty of nature, a slower life, and simpler times can trigger deep, sometimes bittersweet recollections. Identity and heritage weave through these interconnected themes. Moments that create a portrait of self as both an individual and a continuation of family legacy. These poems, woven with memories, offer a nostalgic journey through family, home, and the slow, inevitable changes that time brings.

"To be human is to have a collection of memories that tells you who you are and how you got there."
—*Rosecrans Baldwin*

Heritage

I feel them in my blood,
my ancestors. My body
is their body—cells, molecules,
chromosomes melted and molded
to form me. Celtic and Germanic lines
blurred and blended on American soil
tilled in Appalachian ground until
they grew into something new.

I see their names written
between the Old and New Testaments,
King James written in Elizabethan script.
Faces printed on daguerreotypes
tucked in the Books of Judith
and the Maccabees show the shape
of my eyes, blue, a trait held
in my father's genetic material,
carried from my grandfather.

I want to dive into my DNA
down deep to the core
where my ancestors dwell.
See past the glass darkly,
travel through the dimensions.
I know their future,
                                        they know my past.

Remembering the Farm Girl

Quiet stirs my memory of no cell phones
or streaming TV. My days were spent
watching honeybees gather pollen
from clover growing in the backyard,
listening to cicadas sing in the stillness
of hot summer afternoons. Ninety-degree heat
warming my bones, the sun tanning my skin.

I want to be in those wordless moments again,
see the plants heavy with red heirlooms,
feel the prickly leaves of yellow squash and cucumbers,
pick string beans under the canopy of vines twisting
teepeed poles in rows.

I miss the outdoor kitchen, counter laden
with shucked corncobs scraped clean,
mason jars of creamed corn boiling
in the pressure cooker. Canned tomatoes,
green beans, and peas lining the pantry shelf,
bread and butter pickles sweet on my tongue.

Sweet Harvest

A hawk shadows the lawn,
shades my view
where honeybees hover clover
scattered in the grass, gathering.

Laden with yellow pods of pollen
clinging to their back legs,
I watch them disappear into the hive.

The rusty beehive smoker puffs
as my dad, clad in his sting-proof suit,
walks slowly to the three-tiered honey keeper.

He lifts the metal telescoping roof
to 10 wood frames filled with wax covered goodness,
pulls them out one by one,
and slings the soul of the hive into mason jars.

As I spread the fruits of their labor
on a piece of wheat toast
cradled in my hand,
for a brief moment, I am
surrounded by buzzing, wings fanning
until all that is left
is the pure golden nectar of the gods.

When I Was Eight

I remember waking at dawn one Saturday,
mom and dad still asleep, no alarm
this morning. My sister, her eyes closed, purrs
in the stillness of soft light permeating
our bedroom. I slip from the covers.
Tiptoe to the bathroom. I don't dare flush.
In the kitchen, I down a glass of orange juice
and willing the door not to squeak, sneak
out to the backyard. I sit in a webbed lawn chair
and pull my knees to my ribcage.

Morning smells nice, honeybees suckling clover
still wet with dew. Cicadas, chirping long and low,
drown out the warblers and thrushes.
I trail barefoot to the poplar hoping to find
the dull brown shells they left behind.
Circling the tree, I see three and a line of wood ants
following each other across the trunk and along a root
peeking the surface. A butterfly, fluttering
over squash blossoms, catches my attention—

The back door clicks, screen door slams,
cigarette smoke drifts over my dad as he sips
from a cup of steaming coffee. He catches up
with me in the garden, his familiar scent
mingles with the radishes and green onions.
I walk with him as he checks the beans and tomatoes,
pulls a handful of looseleaf lettuce,
and lays them in my open arms.

Betrayal

I defended them. Spent my summer afternoons
watching them carry their heavy loads
into the square white box and witness their bare legs
as they fly out. We had three hives.
One Dad started from Grandpa's, one he got
from a customer's back deck, and one
that swarmed in the crabapple tree.
They traveled far, miles even, to gather
the nectar of clover and wildwood blooms,
to pack their hind legs with pollen, to fill
the hive with buzzing and toil.
The promise of what would become
inspired me. The work of twelve bees
in just one teaspoon.

When I was eleven, I stepped on a honeybee.
A cold jab shot up my body as the guts
continued to pump poison through
the arch of my bare foot.
My dad scraped the stinger with his fingernail
but the damage was done. I limped
through the screen door, my head throbbing,
hives rising on my arms, legs, and face.
Tears spilling as my eyes swelled shut,
my throat closing, each breath more labored.
Mom rushed me to the hospital. Needles poked
in each arm, each thigh, and a nurse struggled
to connect the IV to the rolling vein in the bend
of my left elbow.

I hid in my room the rest of that summer.
Fall harvest came and went. I didn't watch
the creamy white coating sliced from each frame
or see the gooey goodness cascade
from its waxy comb and flow into mason jars.
Shoes cover my feet when I walk outside,
the call to clover still silent, honey bittered.

Easter Sunday

My memories are thick with ham
and potato salad, frilly dresses
zippered in back, white sweaters
to guard against the chill,
and chocolate crosses.

Prayer book and rosary tucked
in my little purse lined in fake diamonds
and gauzy flowers, I dipped my fingers in the holy water,
made the sign of the cross, always backwards.
I never got my rights and lefts right.

Followed mom to the hard wood pew,
knelt next to grandma and grandpa,
and looked up to Jesus, carved in marble,
hanging on a giant wood cross.

The Long Remembering

I have lived a short time on earth
but have soaked in the stories
and pictures of my ancestors.
Their lineage and heritage
rub into my skin
when I touch heirlooms—

My fingers brush the bedside table
my great-grandfather built.
I drink from my grandmother's teacup,
read God's Word from a 19th century Bible,
a distant aunt's name inscribed on the front.
I lounge on my grandfather's Lincoln-style bed,
an inheritance carried down from his people,
also my people. I look at photographs
of my great-grandmother holding me as a baby.
I can almost feel her arms under me,
smell her breath as she coos and smiles
into my infant face.

My story started before my birth into this life.
It began eons ago all the way back to infinite
beginnings before God created time, before
He spoke the world into existence.
When there was nothing, He knew me.

She Does Everything, Says Nothing

Percolating aroma drifts to my nose,
I wake to coffee grinding,
dress in the clothes she laid out last night,
then go sit at the kitchen table.
She pigtails my hair, fingers twisting each,
leaving a smooth curl dangling
on either side of my face.

Dinner thaws on the counter,
breakfast fries on the stove.
A towel slung over her shoulder,
she forks bacon onto a plate
and lays a handful of Cheerios
on the highchair for baby brother.
Dad slips out the back door.

She slathers mayonnaise on bologna sandwiches,
stuffs them in brown paper bags.
The school bus honks,
she motions for us to hurry.
I watch her button my sister's sweater
as I punch my hands into my jacket,
then she pushes us out the front door.

Planted for Me

I didn't know I would be grateful
for the memory of my pond
where cattails were thick around the edges,
the sun warming my stone lounge,
toes dipped in cool water,
my hair wisping in the breeze.

I didn't know today that my pen
would dance across paper,
sway and swish in cursive, marring
the ivory surface of a once mighty pine
where squirrels twittered and chased,
hid acorns and fallen pecans
in the woods curving
my favorite place to think.

Basic Recipe for Squash

Plant seeds in warm spring soil, four to five,
spaced evenly, in hills six to twelve inches tall.
Sprinkle with water every cloudless morning
and weed each evening when the crickets chirp,
just before the fireflies and the moon rise.

Wait for the cicadas to echo, long and low,
when the mercury reaches near the top
of the thermometer, after squash-bees sway
between blossoms, gathering pollen
and nectar for their offspring.

Pinch each stem just above the crooked neck,
wipe the dirt from their waxy skin, and place
in the harvest basket, the one that once belonged
to grandma. Lay them under a tin roof lean-to
built beside the garden shed.

Heat oil in a cast iron skillet over medium heat.
Slice evenly, cover with cornmeal mix,
and fry golden brown. Serve with sliced tomatoes
still hot from the summer sun, corn on the cob,
fresh baked cornbread, and pork chops, bone in.

Search the Dusty Places

Today, I found a relic of your past,
buried in an old wood box,
cast aside with all the other family treasures.
A faded blue book falling apart
like our family since you left this world.

My fingers trace the gold letters on the cover, *My Poetry Book,
an Anthology of Modern Verse for Boys and Girls.*
I fan the aged pages looking for your scribbles,
like the faded ones in the small New Testament
you carried during World War II. I find none.

I heard you were a lover of poetry,
often writing some, although none survived.
Would you like my poetry?

You taught me playfulness
and indifference,
but you gave me so much more—
your name, piercing blue eyes,
intelligence, ingenuity, and artistry.

I wish I knew you better, Grandpa,
but maybe I do, more so than I think
because a part of you was given to me,
your words, infused with mine,
finally written for all to read.

Birthplace

I beckon *My Old Kentucky Home*, the Commonwealth, the Iroquois'
land of tomorrow. North blurring into the South. I hear the twang
of bluegrass in horse country, Lexington's Legacy. Bill Monroe.

I crave Kentucky Fried Chicken. Jim Beam. Mint juleps
and wide-brim hats. I miss running barefoot in Appalachia,
spun honey dripping from beehive frames. Smores.

I recall Saturday softball games with a Louisville Slugger.
Underground passages snaking thru Mammoth Cave.
Camping at Laurel Lake and Dale Hollow. College basketball.

I picture cardinals nesting in tulip poplars. Goldenrod thick
along the highway. The Cumberland Plateau, Daniel Boone,
and coonskin hats. Fort Knox. The coal miner's daughter.

Dad's Pipe

The chipped mouthpiece sits between his teeth
as he strikes the flint, eyes focused on the flame
from the Zippo. With each draw in, the fire
disappears into the chamber, charring
the top layer of cherry tobacco. Smoke shadows
his tanned face with each puff.
                              I watch the ritual
every night after supper, hands elbow deep in suds.
The kettle whistles, Mom pours him a cup of tea,
sweetens it with honey from our hives, three,
nestled under the crabapple tree in the backyard.
The bees are clustering now, shivering to generate heat,
surrounded in sweetness under the Cold Moon.

Cherry scent from the plug-in drifts
across the kitchen as I load the dishwasher.
I remember his blue-collar shirt smudged in grease
and hard work. His calloused fingers holding the pipe
as he flipped through the newspaper. I make a cup
of hot tea, sweeten it with honey from a local beekeeper
and scroll through social media.
                              The same ritual,
same movements, different generations. Our cells clustered
in each other, moving together through time. I pick up his lighter,
the one I gave him many Christmases ago, run my thumb
over his initials, flick it open and strike the flint three times.
Only sparks, the fluid long dried up.

In the Middle of Things

Some of them are gone now.
Those who shaped my life,
living only in my thoughts, my heart.

Memories jumble, blend with every day,
glimpses like photographs,
sometimes moving, sometimes still.

My life starts
the day after Christmas
during the Vietnam conflict

after man landed on the moon
in the house my mom and dad owned
out past the edge of town.

Honeysuckle thick along the back fence,
chasing my dachshund Fonzie.
Sharing a room with my sister,
epic fights on that pink shag carpet.

Dad's pipe and cherry tobacco,
mom's hash made with leftover roast,
ice skating on the lake at grandma and grandpa's.

Wisps of cells, interlocking us in heritage,
life forced forward by time,
held hostage to aging.

Carrying all of us to the next phase—
that unknown place we long to visit.
Just not tomorrow.

Scent of Smoke

A feathered barrette pinned to her hair
and braided leather across her forehead,
my cousin, tired of babysitting, drags me
and my sister to the woods to meet up
with her friends, smoking cigarettes,
sneaking swigs of Jack, threatening us
not to tell. I would beg for a puff, a sip.
They laughed when I coughed and gagged.

I still smell the smoke—cigarettes, cigars,
sometimes the other stuff. Flashes of my uncle,
always with a cigar between his fingers.
My dad, his pipe hanging out of his mouth,
friends chain smoking. I can even feel the draw
of the Winston Lights I used to smoke.

It's funny what you remember. The scents
and sights that trigger them. I watched a video
my cousin posted to social media. Her parents,
dancing. He has dementia now. The body remembers
even if the mind does not. I wonder
                                    if he remembers me.

Camping at Dale Hollow Lake

We pitched the tent on Cactus Island
beside a Boy Scout camp whose
morning reveille woke us at six every morning.

Mom always packed bologna just for me,
(I hate peanut butter and jelly.)
well, for dad too. We ate them while fishing for supper,
bass and crappie to cook over an open fire.

My sister and I float in the lake, feet dangling,
fish nibbling our toes. My brother stacks rocks
on the shoreline, mom reading Agatha Christie,
and dad scraping fish.

The beach was sharp, flat stones, not yet sand.
Pondweed threatened to tangle my legs, so I swam faster,
kicked harder thinking it couldn't grab hold.

Every Visit to the Dry Cleaners

I see the mirage of you, grandpa,
through the hot, steamy shop
reared back in your squeaky metal chair
behind that old wood desk.

Dry cleaning fluid sparks memories
of bear hugs, silly jokes, and quarters for candy bars.
You were my fun, my favorite
and no one knew, not even you.

I told you "I love you" once.
You were at the kitchen table,
in your last days.
I whispered it in your ear,
unrehearsed,
from my heart.
You were stoic.
I was crushed.

I pay for my clean London Fog raincoat
wrapped in plastic and look forward
to the next time.

He Says Nothing, Does Everything

Shaken awake at 4 am, I dress in the dark,
down the glass of orange juice on the kitchen table,
and stomp into my rubber boots at the back door.
Pigtails lopsided, I crawl into the front seat.
Dad latches the boat to the truck.

Diesel engine vibrating, we sit at the red light,
his tanned face illuminated by the dashboard
and mine looking out the passenger's side window.
Solitary figures under streetlights
fading in the early dawn.

Sunlight cracks the horizon,
flashes between trees
as we zig zag the rolling hills
frosted in last night's dew,
passing hay bales and red angus,
their breath warming the air.

The lake—still, wisps of fog
hovering the surface, cow lilies
hugging the edge. I spot
a turtle on a flat rock
partially hidden in the bulrushes
and blue flag irises. Frogs croak
in protest as the trailer eases
backwards, tires displacing the gravel
that disappears into the water.

Our fishing boat ripples the quiet cove,
trolling motor humming toward a good spot.
He chases a minnow with his fingers,
pins one to my hook and tosses the bait
into the water. I watch the cork
as Dad hands me hot chocolate,
straightens my pigtails,
and zips my coat to my chin.

When Daffodils Sing

I am drawn to yesteryear,
to the backyard of my childhood
where bees hum, and our dogs whimper
to be let out of their pen. The garden dormant,
still bland and brown with piles of plants, rotten
from last year's harvest. I hear the call of wrens,
of coyotes shedding their winter coats,
fur scattered in the field near my pond.

Oh to be in those moments again,
where Dad surveys the grass, the garden,
pipe clutched between his teeth,
deciding the first mow, the first till
into the softening ground. The beagles itch
to chase rabbits and squirrels.
Our honeybees prepare to swarm,
virgin queens emerge for the mating dance.

Spring Libations

Pollen breezes a yellow dusting
and coats my sinuses. Warm honey sweetens
my tastebuds and whiskey soothes my throat,
lemon and cinnamon, a calm melody.

The aroma of the hot toddy
carries me back to the kitchen of my childhood
with Dad puffing his pipe, Mom putting the kettle on,
and crickets crooning through the screen door.

Dusk dims the day and I watch the dogs
lounging in their pen, the beehives
busy with brood-rearing, and the freshly tilled ground,
ready for planting, disappear into the night.

Yesterday Echoes

Cinder blocks stack and rise on the nine acres
where orchard grass was once cut into hay bales.
Progress grows, choking out the meadow
lined in birch and boxelder. My pond lays dormant,
stagnant between white-lined asphalt, too hot for hoofs
and paws to walk across for a drink.

Forty years dim and shade the landscape
from forest to field to factory. Forklifts skitter
where deer, coyotes, and rabbits once foraged,
nested, and raised their young. The country road
swells to a four-lane highway squeezed
between Home Depot and Walmart.

I remember cars whispering past
on hot summer afternoons.
Crickets and cicadas drowning out Mom
calling me for dinner. The poplar I climbed
every day for ten years still stands
on a patch of grass next to the dumpsters.
Cardboard boxes crushed and bundled in stacks
where Dad rested after picking beans in the garden.

The frozen food aisle smells of BBQ on the grill
and honeysuckle that grew along our back fence.
I hear honeybee hives buzz and hum at the meat counter.
Ambient music plays *Every Breath You Take*
from my record collection.

The checkout aisle was once the back porch
where me and my sister had watermelon
spitting contests every summer.
Our swing set looms in my mind's eye
next to the cart return. I see my baby brother
swinging, giggling, chain screeching.

Under the Swing Set

I poke a stick into the brown mound
of sifted earth. Black ants appear
and swarm toward me. I giggle
as they march up my legs to explore
my orange and pink flowered sundress.

I call daddy to come see.
He drops the hammer,
spits nails out of his mouth,
and roughly brushes the ants
from my three-year-old body.

He swings me high in the air,
hugs me, and plops me
back on my feet. Scolds me
for I don't know what, then
pushes me to the back porch
where mom sits snapping beans.

Canning

Pickle juice simmering on the stove
perfumes the kitchen, late summer cucumbers
and beets, sliced and quartered, fill all available bowls.
Jars, lids, and bands sanitized and ready to be filled.

The television blares the life of penguins
and I search my memory for winter: that day in April
when four inches of snow suffused the parking lot
at my high school, my fingers numb and raw from scraping
the windshield. They didn't close school in those days.
We just plowed through.

The timer dings. I pull jars of dill pickles
from the water bath, line them on the cooling rack
lost in yesterday's kitchen when Mom canned
freshly picked green beans and Dad harvested honey
from our hives. I can still hear the bees humming.

Abandoned to the Interstate

Dark clouds hang low
over the hollowed-out building
and Shell gas pumps. Weeds thrive
in the cracks and crevices
of the faded asphalt parking lot.

Concrete posts, flaking yellow,
guard the long-ago gas price
clinging to the fuel station
layered in age and black mold.

The sign, peeling with memories,
looms over the once thriving truck stop.
I can still hear dishes clanging,
jukebox playing *East Bound and Down*,
and truckers flirting with the waitresses.

Dad and I always stopped before every fishing trip
to eat eggs, bacon, biscuits and gravy.
Under halogen lamps, he filled the van and the boat,
checked the oil and cleaned the windshield.

Home Remedy

My body hurled last night's dinner,
fever tipping one hundred two degrees,
and I am alone.
              In my delirium,
I feel her presence, cool hand
on my forehead, her silhouette shadowing
the room, my room, in my grownup house
where I am trying to be brave.
              I remember her
home remedies, hot Jell-O—cherry—my favorite,
and saltines around a steaming mug, The only thing
that stays down.
              The next morning,
I wake to birds singing, the storm of last night over,
and a cup and saucer on my nightstand,
                    only crumbs remain.

Traces of Her

Before dawn, before the sky highlights
treetops and power lines. Before the blue
blues the morning, my headlights show me the road.
I can only see a few feet in front of me
but I know the way, have traveled it many times.
The dashboard casts a soft glow on my face.
I glance at my eyes in the visor mirror,
still bloodshot from inserting contacts too early.

I hit the freeway, going north. I will stop
just before the Ohio River to visit Mom.
She doesn't know I am coming.
She doesn't keep up with much lately,
always asking the same questions when I visit.
How long are you staying? Are you staying with me?
She knows me, her oldest daughter,
but she lives in the moment, not grasping
what comes next or where she was an hour ago.

On the drive up, I prepare myself,
reminding that dementia does not define
who she was or is today. We drive around town,
talk about the past, what she remembers.
I see glimmers every now and then
when she punches through
the brawn of a disease that holds her captive
and she tells me what she had for breakfast.

Suppertime

Whiffs of pot roast simmering
in the crockpot greet me
when I get home from work.
A vision of Grandma, her thinning
white hair and wrinkled skin,
spooning meat juices over the roast
sails into my memory.

I stepped down, tripped across the illusion
of her kitchen, the linoleum floor, and
almost crashed into her white metal cabinets
and Formica countertops. Grandpa sat
at his usual spot in front of the window.
I can still see the sheer white curtains
tied back in crisscross fashion,
the gauzy view of the garden,
where the steamy bowl of kale came from.

Ready to eat? My husband asks.
Snapped back to the present,
only the aroma of pot roast remains.

Monday in May

I drove by my old elementary school today,
remember weaving silk ribbons over and under
the other girls in frilly dresses round and round
the Maypole. The little tomboy, I was called, dirt
under my fingernails that could grow potatoes,
with Tinker Bell lip gloss and scraped knees.

I miss that girl sometimes, the one who climbed trees,
played softball, and shot bow and arrows dead center
on hay targets. Fished minnows out of the bucket,
dug for nightcrawlers, caught fireflies in mason jars,
and watched honeybees gather pollen for hours
                                              and hours.

Buried Driveway

Cars and trucks race back and forth
on the highway, flickering my view.
Rewinding memories all the way back.

Red brick, square, shingled roof.
Picture windows framed in black shutters
on either side of the oak door
with three stair-step windowpanes.
Boxwood shrubs line the front
between the wall and the walk.

I can still see my childhood home
among the sea of pre-owned cars
in the parking lot that was once a front lawn.
Faint ghost-like remembrances
of picking dandelions, playing in puddles
left after hard rains, and Hook Man,
wearing his reminder of Vietnam,
walking me home when I wandered
to Miss Ruby's for chocolate chip cookies.

There it is. The entrance to the driveway
still clinging to the road, an unmarked grave
of memories buried under asphalt.
An unassuming reminder of a family
that once lived there.

In Appreciation

To my writing community—fellow poets and friends—thank you for your insight, inspiration, and generous spirit. Your voices have helped me refine my own.

A special note of gratitude to my monthly poetry group:
Helga Kidder, KB Ballentine, Camille Burkley,
Rachel Landrum Crumble, Cynthia Young, and Karen Phillips.
Your thoughtful feedback and unwavering support have helped me grow as a poet.

With deep appreciation to my mentors and dear friends,
KB Ballentine and Helga Kidder—thank you for recognizing the writer in me before I did. Your encouragement, wisdom, and guidance were instrumental in bringing this collection to life.

And to my husband—my love, my inspiration, and the one who loves me so well—thank you for being my constant.

Chris Wood has a sense of wonder and respect for heritage and the evolving power of words. From her childhood in Kentucky and currently residing in Tennessee, she draws inspiration from Southern landscapes, etymology, and Appalachian life. Her debut collection, *Yesterday Echoes*, is a barefoot walk through memory with the pulse of generations in her veins, and a reminder that the sacred often hides in the simplest things.

Her poetry appears in numerous journals and publications including *American First Magazine, Salvation South, Dandelion Scribes, Lothlorien Poetry Journal, Heart of Flesh Literary Journal, Lit Shark Magazine. Her work is also in several anthologies,* including *Women Speak* (2025), *Bayou, Blues, & Red Clay Poetry Anthology* (2024), *Nothing Divine Dies: The Poetry of Nature* (2022), and *Adult Children* (2021).

Chris is also the author of *Word Vignettes: Unraveling the History Behind Every Word*, and lives with her husband and a lively household of fur-babies, where she balances her writing life with a fulfilling career as a Director in Operations Services for a real estate investment trust. She specializes in tenant billing for shopping centers—a role she approaches with the same precision and curiosity that shapes her literary work. She is a member of the Tennessee Mountain Writers, Chattanooga Writers' Guild, and Poetry Society of Tennessee. Learn more at *https://chriswoodwriter.com.*

You can also find her on—
Facebook: @chriswoodwriter
https://www.facebook.com/chriswoodwriter/

Instagram: @chriswoodwriter
https://www.instagram.com/chriswoodwriter/

X: @chriswoodpoet
https://x.com/chriswoodpoet

Pinterest: @chriswoodwriter
https://pin.it/3NCE0H8ZD

www.ingramcontent.com/pod-product-compliance
Lightning Source LLC
Chambersburg PA
CBHW022049080426
42734CB00009B/1287